© **Bring Home Happiness**
BY SANDEEP RAVIDUTT SHARMA

Table of Contents

Foreword IV

Bring Home Happiness 1

© **Bring Home Happiness**
BY SANDEEP RAVIDUTT SHARMA

Foreword

This book provides you with a list of 100 motivational quotes and thoughts about LIFE, churned out by my mind with the consciousness, grace and energy of **Shiva Shakti**. I'm sure if you keep reading, referring, sharing these thoughts and quotes about LIFE, you may derive inspiration and develop good understanding of various perspectives and facts. You may explore the world to bring home happiness but ultimately will find it right within your heart.

"Your positive thoughts, kindness and humility are good enough to bring home happiness."

I sincerely hope, you will find this book amazing, interesting, rejuvenating, unique and a constant source of inspiration.

Thank You and Happy Reading.

© Bring Home Happiness
BY SANDEEP RAVIDUTT SHARMA

© Copyright 2018 Sandeep Ravidutt Sharma - All rights reserved. In no way is it legal to reproduce, duplicate, or transmit any part of this document in either electronic means or in printed format. Recording of this publication is strictly prohibited and any storage of this document is not allowed unless with written permission from the publisher. All rights reserved. The information provided herein is stated to be truthful and consistent, in that any liability, in terms of inattention or otherwise, by any usage or abuse of any policies, processes, or directions contained within is the solitary and utter responsibility of the recipient reader. Under no circumstances will any legal responsibility or blame be held against the author / publisher for any reparation, damages, or monetary loss due to the information herein, either directly or indirectly. The author own all copyrights.

Legal Notice: This book is copyright protected. This is only for personal use. You cannot amend, distribute, sell, use, quote or paraphrase any part or the content within this book without the consent of the author or copyright owner. Legal action will be pursued if this is breached.

Disclaimer Notice: Please note the information contained within this book is for motivational, educational and knowledge sharing purpose only. Every attempt has been made to provide the reader accurate, up to date and reliable complete information. No warranties of any kind are expressed or implied. Readers acknowledge that the author is not engaging in the rendering of legal, financial, medical or professional advice. By reading this document, the reader agrees that under no circumstances the author / publisher is responsible for any losses, direct or indirect, which are incurred as a result of the use of information contained within this document, including, but not limited to, — errors, omissions, or inaccuracies.

Cover photo designed by: Ms Bhagyashri Sharma

If you have further questions, contact on **Tel: +919969256731**
Email: sandeepraviduttsharma@gmail.com

© Bring Home Happiness
BY SANDEEP RAVIDUTT SHARMA

Dedication

This book is dedicated to **Shiva Shakti** - the epitome of love. Lord Shiva is pure consciousness symbolising the masculine principle. Goddess Shakti symbolises the active feminine energy of Shiva and is synonymously identified with **Tripura Sundari, Sati** or **Parvati**.

These primal principles are also called as PURUSHA representing consciousness and PRAKRITI denoting the nature. Shiva and Shakti are manifestations of the all-in-one divine consciousness. Shiva is the paternal love of God that gives us consciousness, knowledge and clarity. Shakti is the motherly love of God that showers warmth, care and ensures our protection. Shiva and Shakti exist within each of us as the masculine and feminine energy. To please **Shiva Shakti** praying for the well being, love, happiness, strength, positive energy and success of my readers in their life, I hereby recite the following mantra...

"**Sarva Mangala Mangalye Shive Sarvartha Sadhike Sharanye Tryambake Gauri Narayani Namostute**"

Bring home happiness

© **Bring Home Happiness**
BY SANDEEP RAVIDUTT SHARMA

You can't afford to sit idle when you face life challenge.

© **Bring Home Happiness**
BY SANDEEP RAVIDUTT SHARMA

Your inner peace determines your outlook. Stay calm and joyful.

© **Bring Home Happiness**
BY SANDEEP RAVIDUTT SHARMA

Hope keeps coming back to meet the efforts wanting to see dear Win.

Nothing reflects better than the light.

© **Bring Home Happiness**
BY SANDEEP RAVIDUTT SHARMA

Trouble is no more when you look at it and smile.

Find ways to Live and let live with freedom.

Joy of winning reflects in your voice and Smile.

Inefficient ones always seek someone to blame. Expose them in time and make them accountable.

Live each moment of joy now instead of savouring it for tomorrow.

Our lives may change by just a single decision. Think positive and choose wisely.

© **Bring Home Happiness**
BY SANDEEP RAVIDUTT SHARMA

Feeling insecure is natural but building a secured environment need best efforts.

© **Bring Home Happiness**
BY SANDEEP RAVIDUTT SHARMA

Real friends never give up on you even when you have decided to quit.

Stay true to your commitment, and you can build trust.

© **Bring Home Happiness**
BY SANDEEP RAVIDUTT SHARMA

Walk a while always with a smile.

Fire of knowledge can light or burn. It depends on who holds and how it is applied.

Communicate your noble intentions well and you get many hands raised to support your cause.

Self-belief comes with knowledge and experience.

Happiness and sorrow are twins separated at birth. Both comes to meet you one after the other.

Light your lamp today.
Tomorrow is another day.

© Bring Home Happiness
BY SANDEEP RAVIDUTT SHARMA

Redeem your kindness in favour of a smile back.

Everyone is a hero in his own story and way.

Stop interfering in the lives of the other if you find your counseling is falling on deaf ears. Time has got answer for everyone and everything.

© **Bring Home Happiness**
BY SANDEEP RAVIDUTT SHARMA

Wishes are many but focus can be only on one that gets fulfilled.

Positivity enhances the beauty of your life.

© **Bring Home Happiness**
BY SANDEEP RAVIDUTT SHARMA

Your efforts influence your fate. Keep Going.

Build a bridge to connect diversities.

You cannot plug and play relationship. It's a string of love which both needs to hold firmly from their end.

Plant the seed of love, and you get to see flowers of happiness waving at you.

Unclutter your mind and welcome beautiful thoughts.

The glow on your face and beautiful smile are enough to tell how much love and kindness do you have in your heart.

Be ready to fight someday to ensure peace.

Be anxious to find solutions and not to discuss problems.

Liberate your mind from the slavery of your desires by deciding what's essential, and the one's that can wait or discarded.

It was not worth reading, if you can't make out the moral of the story. Or is it that you need to improve upon your understanding. Think over.

Great day starts with you.

Welcome amazing thoughts if you like to live in an amazing world.

Run your business to earn profits and grow but not with the intention to downsize your competitors.

Your action is the convergence of your thought, plan, knowledge, experience and strong resolve to achieve. Take timely action.

© **Bring Home Happiness**
BY SANDEEP RAVIDUTT SHARMA

You think you are born to win. That's fine till the time you are making efforts.

Noble intention doesn't need too much of convincing.

Look forward when you want to reach your destination. Turn back only when someone who is left behind cries for your help.

Accept what comes your way if nothing is working as per your plan.

Just by closing your eyes you can't shut down the world. Face it and cheer for challenges.

Those who are eager to reach their destination hardly know that it's just a stopover for the next one.

© **Bring Home Happiness**
BY SANDEEP RAVIDUTT SHARMA

Together with Love we can create a beautiful world and live in harmony.

© **Bring Home Happiness**
BY SANDEEP RAVIDUTT SHARMA

Discover yourself in the mirror of confidence, and you can see a winner in the making.

Wonderful are the ways of the Lord. He makes you scale Everest but on reaching atop fills your mind with longing for the ground.

Thinking beyond what is already known can let you discover a new world.

Don't quit unless you have tried.

© **Bring Home Happiness**
BY SANDEEP RAVIDUTT SHARMA

Beautiful mind creates the amazing world on the canvas of life.

Abandon your shyness and hesitation if it fails you in life.

Challenges are eager to meet one who knows how to convert them into an opportunity.

Great minds don't just see beautiful dreams but convert them into reality.

Speak up your mind or else you will lose the opportunity.

The mask will come out soon for those who have learned how to pretend.

Whatever happens in this world is as per the wish of the Lord. His wish is our command.

Nobody ever settles in life. Without challenges life doesn't exist.

Tag your happiness with words of joy, amazement and gratitude.

External motivation can work once you have inner motivation in the activation mode.

People meet for a reason which unfolds gradually. Give your best, and you may get the best.

Motivation harnesses your ability and attitude ensures how you win.

© **Bring Home Happiness**
BY SANDEEP RAVIDUTT SHARMA

Let your laughter outlive your achievement through your celebration.

© **Bring Home Happiness**
BY SANDEEP RAVIDUTT SHARMA

Sometimes life makes you stand at the crossroads and prompt you to choose either quenching your thirst or feeding the hunger.

Explore new ways to solve old issues.

You are free to think.

Live your dreams by working it out.

Treat others the way you want them to treat you.

© **Bring Home Happiness**
BY SANDEEP RAVIDUTT SHARMA

Long live the kindness and hope.

Take it forward if you are convinced about the noble intention.

© **Bring Home Happiness**
BY SANDEEP RAVIDUTT SHARMA

Let your tears flow out but keep the courage within.

Keep moving forward in life whether you win or lose.

Only when you lose, the true value of what you had in life comes to the fore.

Nobody can really understand your pain and loss. Find courage to rise again.

© **Bring Home Happiness**
BY SANDEEP RAVIDUTT SHARMA

Allow your mind to absorb the goodness all around and help you to maintain positive attitude at all times.

© **Bring Home Happiness**
BY SANDEEP RAVIDUTT SHARMA

Encouraging words many a times makes a winner of tomorrow out of losers of today.

© **Bring Home Happiness**
BY SANDEEP RAVIDUTT SHARMA

The fragrance of friendship goes beyond the Ocean and returns back with an air of love.

Accept the change gracefully or make attempt to lead the change for the good.

Take charge of your life, and you can cross over the tide.

Self awareness comes from your observation and deep involvement.

Make attempt to understand before passing any judgement about the other.

Knowledge empowers you but remembers to power the world.

© **Bring Home Happiness**
BY SANDEEP RAVIDUTT SHARMA

Fence sitters can only comment what should have been done. It's the player on the ground who kicks to win.

© Bring Home Happiness
BY SANDEEP RAVIDUTT SHARMA

Instead of spending time in complaining, it's better to educate and make others understand your perspective.

© **Bring Home Happiness**
BY SANDEEP RAVIDUTT SHARMA

Life struggle tries to push you down but it's your strong resolve that helps you to win.

Learning is life and life is learning throughout.

Leave behind trail of knowledge for others to learn and follow.

The tone of your words speaks a lot about whether you are here to resolve or wage a war.

© **Bring Home Happiness**
BY SANDEEP RAVIDUTT SHARMA

Withdraw your application if money has replaced talent as the eligibility criteria.

© **Bring Home Happiness**
BY SANDEEP RAVIDUTT SHARMA

Fortunate are the ones who get to see the rainbow of happiness. Remember your deeds create your fortune.

Don't encourage favouritism of any kind if you want to select a winning combination.

Laugh it out if you are in pain. Laugh it in if you are happy. Remember to laugh in any case.

Beautiful dreams wake you up to achieve them.

Let excitement live another day.

Don't try to find meaning when someone cracks a joke.

It doesn't matter if you have lost today. Your presence in the next race matters the most.

You can always find room in your heart or house when it's matter of your liking.

Step forward without any hesitation when you no longer care about the result of your actions.

Your wet feet is proof enough that you have touched the shore.

It's good to play right for the first time but you will never know what goes in the mind of those who failed.

Prepare well for your next mission instead of spending time in finding faults in the mission itself.

www.ingramcontent.com/pod-product-compliance
Lightning Source LLC
Chambersburg PA
CBHW031441210526
45464CB00005B/2291